How to Keep Going
When You Want to Give Up

By Martin Meadows

To Donnie:

High School Graduation

2016

Hal & Pam Pray

Download This Book in Other Formats

I want to thank you for buying my book and offer you access to my book in three additional formats: MOBI, EPUB and PDF.

Click the link below to receive it:

http://www.profoundselfimprovement.com/grit

In addition to getting "Grit," you'll also have an opportunity to get my new books for free, enter giveaways and receive other valuable emails from me.

Again, here's the link to sign up:

http://www.profoundselfimprovement.com/grit

Contents

Prologue

If you browse through the interviews with some of the most successful people on Earth, you'll find one common piece of advice shared by virtually all of them:

They never give up on their big goals.

Research shows that grit is a better predictor for success than any other factor[i]. The ability to keep going despite setbacks is more important than your IQ, character or other external factors like your upbringing or surroundings.

But what does it really mean to "never give up"? What exactly is grit? How do you persevere when faced with larger than life difficulties? How do you keep going when you're at the brink of exhaustion and all your hard work hasn't been rewarded yet?

I wrote this book to explore the subject of persistence from a more scientific point of view than cliché self-help sayings. I want to share with you how exactly to stick to your goals according to the peak performers and science – not vague motivational advice that claims we have unlimited strength once we're motivated enough.

By making it the goal of this book, I assume you already have a powerful motivation to work on your goals, yet you find yourself rapidly approaching the point of giving up. Together we'll explore how to push through obstacles and stay tough even when you've yet to get the taste of the reward you're after.

I supplement scientific advice with my personal experience in various areas such as fitness, business and learning new skills. Some of the things I achieved thanks to persistence include losing over 30 pounds in 12 weeks (and no, I've never gained it back), creating several businesses, learning two foreign languages, and overcoming crippling shyness.

We'll start with asking the most important question (nothing else matters if your answer to this question is "no"), and then proceed to seven chapters dedicated to various aspects of persistence. In the final chapter, you'll get advice from six other self-help authors to get different perspectives.

When you finish this book, you'll possess a whole slew of tips and tricks to keep going when you want to give up. You'll understand which behaviors will threaten your goals and which ones will help you stay on course.

Last but not least, you'll be ready to tackle challenges that would make an average person yell with frustration.

Chapter 1: Should You Even Keep Going?

Grit serves you no purpose if you're performing the wrong action. Blind persistence sometimes holds you back from achieving your goals.

Bestselling author Seth Godin points out in his book "The Dip: The Extraordinary Benefits of Knowing When to Quit (and When to Stick)"[ii] that if you're not going to put in the effort to do your best, you might as well quit.

Consequently, the most important question you should ask yourself before you even start learning how to keep going is, "Should I even keep going or should I give up?" If you want to find the correct answer to this question, we first need to explore the concept of "the dip" a little bit more.

Understanding the Dip

The graph below illustrates the concept of the dip:

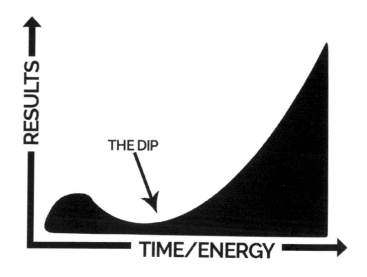

When you start out, you enjoy a short-term period of rapid growth. You lose your first couple of pounds, you make your first sale, you say your first sentence in a foreign language, or you drive the first mile on a motorcycle.

After the initial gratifying period, things get harder. You no longer improve so quickly, or even worse – you feel stuck, unable to push through the obstacles.

In his book, Seth Godin says that if something is worth doing, there's probably a dip to experience. The dip creates scarcity, which in turn leads to exceptional value possessed by the few people who endure it.

The longer you endure the dip, the closer you are to success. Yet, most people who have found themselves in the dip give up before they can get out of it.

In some cases, they make the right decision. They save time and effort they would otherwise spend on something they shouldn't have been doing in the first place. In other cases, they throw away all the progress they have made so far.

How do you decide whether you should give up or keep going? There are several questions to ask.

When Should You Give Up?

Quitting in the dip usually seems like a bad idea (after all, you've already invested a lot of time and effort into doing something). However, we humans don't act as rationally as we think. Persistence isn't always the answer to all your problems.

Before you skip this chapter and tell yourself you *surely* shouldn't quit, consider the sunk cost fallacy. If you believe in a "Don't waste" philosophy (as most adults do), you're affected by this bias (but as studies point out, children are not[iii]).

Let's say you went to the college, but one year later you're no longer motivated to keep going. The decision to quit would make more sense than forcing yourself to do something for which you no longer have enthusiasm. Yet, most people would consider the year spent studying too large of an investment to quit. They think of it as a waste of resources. Even though staying at the college would lead to even more waste, many people would irrationally keep going.

Consequently, the first question you should ask yourself is whether you want to keep going just because of what you've already invested. If it's your primary (or worse, sole) motivation, chances are you'd be much better off quitting right now.

Seth Godin argues that if you're not invested enough to become the best in the world in what you're trying to achieve, you might as well quit. If you're settling for mediocrity, the decision to quit will benefit you more than merely trying to be "okay" at something.

Bestselling author and multimillionaire Richard Koch points out in his book "Living the 80/20 Way"[iv] that the key to success is to limit your focus to things that mirror your individuality. You can't be the best at everything, and persistence pays the biggest dividends when you focus on what you're truly best at.

Koch's and Godin's approach is valid for people who want to achieve big career goals. However, it doesn't necessarily apply to smaller goals like learning a foreign language or learning another side skill where the objective isn't to become a world-class performer.

Before you quit because you realize you can't be the best in the world in what you want to achieve, ask yourself why you're doing it. Perhaps you'll never become a proficient Spanish speaker, but your basic communication skills will suffice you enough to travel Spanish-speaking countries. If, on the other hand, your goal is to become surgeon, but you're not so fired up you want to become the best in the world, do yourself (and others) a favor and give up now.

The last thing to consider when making the decision to keep going or give up is to ask yourself if you still have enthusiasm – both for the process and for the goal.

There's a difference between short-term discouragement (which happens to most, if not all successful people) and long-term lack of enthusiasm and loss of the entire vision. If your vision no longer fires you up (and it's not the result of your current struggles, but something entirely else), the decision to quit is likely to turn out more beneficial than sticking to it.

A Couple of Examples of When I Gave Up (and Made the Right Choice)

To help you better understand how to quit strategically, I will share with you several examples from my life.

Many successful people I admire are capable of programming, so I figured it could be a useful skill to develop. I enrolled in a programming course and invested several days in learning the basics of programming. What was fun in the beginning soon

13

turned into something extremely confusing and frustrating.

I quit several days later when I realized technology has never been my forte and my strengths lay somewhere else. If I knew what I know now, I wouldn't have even started. There was no chance I would go past mediocrity. In fact, it was extremely unlikely I would understand even the basics of programming. It lay so far outside my expertise, skill set, and interests, it was a project destined for failure.

The realistic end goal (being an average programmer) wouldn't satisfy me, so quitting was a better choice.

Another example related to programming was my idea to run a software-dependent company. It started out well, but even though the idea had a lot of potential, I couldn't find enough enthusiasm to keep going. It's hard to grow a business if you can't get fired up to provide value to your clients.

Several people told me I should keep going since I already invested a considerable amount of money and time into this project. I decided against listening to them and gave up. I freed up time and energy to focus on a completely unrelated project that turned out to be a much better fit that played off my strengths.

I couldn't have been happier with my decision.

Every author will tell you that the hardest part of writing a book is the middle of the story. It's where most writers get stuck, some of them to never finish their first work.

I also quit on several of my stories, but I also had several books where I went past this phase. The difference was the story and the characters – the "why" of the book.

If I knew where the story was going and liked my characters, I could push through the hardest part of writing when you bang your head against the wall in frustration. If I didn't have the entire vision in mind, I figured it was better to quit. If I wasn't enthusiastic enough to keep writing it, no reader would be enthusiastic enough to read it, either.

SHOULD YOU EVEN KEEP GOING? QUICK RECAP

1. The dip is the moment when you experience little reward and lack motivation to keep going. The longer you persevere during this phase, the closer you are to success. Everybody experiences the dip when working on something worthwhile. There's no workaround.

2. The sunk cost fallacy can make you keep going when it's better to give up. If your sole motivation to stick to your goals is to not lose what you've already invested, you might be better off giving up.

3. If you're not willing to do your best but expect extraordinary results, give up now. It's a waste of time to be mediocre while you could work on something you're great at.

4. If you no longer have the passion for your goal, give up. Don't mistake short-term discouragement with lack of enthusiasm, though. If you've been working on your goals for several weeks with little to no enjoyment, it's probably no longer the right goal for you.

Chapter 2: Routines – the Key to Persistence

You can accomplish a lot in your life with sheer persistence, but there's no reason to rely on your grit alone. When you support it with daily routines, which require little to no effort to perform, you'll free up a lot of willpower to use in other areas of your life.

Why are routines so important and how do you introduce them into your life to persevere no matter the circumstances? That's what we're going to explore in this chapter.

What You Can Learn from the First People Who Reached the South Pole

In 1911, two teams of explorers set out to reach the South Pole. One of the teams was led by Roald Amundsen, who set a consistent goal for his team. The other team was led by Robert Falcon Scott, who let the external factors and his feelings lead to the tragic outcome of his and his team's journey.

Amundsen decided to follow a simple routine – each day, he and his team had to travel on average 15 nautical miles per day. It was a realistic pace; not too exhausting, and not too easy, either. No matter the weather (except extreme conditions), he and his team traveled for no more (and no less) than 15 to 20 nautical miles. The rest of the time, he and his team rested in their sleeping bags.

Scott, on the other hand, drove his team to exhaustion when the weather was good and didn't leave his tent when the weather was ugly. He believed that the efforts don't count until you tax yourself completely.

Amundsen and his team reached the South Pole first – and returned a couple of months later to tell the tale. Scott and his team died on their way back – left without strength for a much more arduous return journey.

There's no doubt that both men were persistent. It was no easy feat (and still isn't) to reach the South Pole on foot. Yet, it was Amundsen who succeeded – thanks to strategic persistence and the power of proper rest, not because of pushing him and his team as hard as possible.

When I'm writing a book, I have a simple routine – no matter what happens, I have to write 3,000 words per day. Even if I accomplish nothing else during the day, I consider it a productive day of work and feel good about what I've achieved.

I don't spend hours thinking whether I want to write or not. I've made writing 3,000 words a part of my daily routine that happens in pretty much the same way as brushing my teeth.

I never make exceptions and write less – unless I'm writing the last words in the book. I also don't write much more than 3000 words, as I know it's a sure-fire way to burn out.

The daunting process of writing a book becomes much easier when it's broken into smaller steps repeated every single day as an automatic behavior.

This simple habit allows me to write up to ten times faster than other authors who write when they feel like doing it. Waiting for inspiration doesn't work for me. Neither does it work for Stephen King, who wrote in his book "On Writing,"[v] "Amateurs sit and wait for inspiration, the rest of us just get up and go to work."

Make Your Life Easier by Establishing Daily Routines

Each day you wake up, you head to the bathroom and brush your teeth. Do you need persistence to keep doing it? Do you skip it when you don't feel well? Do you whine you have to do it every single day?

Brushing your teeth is one of your habits. All of us have dozens, if not hundreds, of both little and big habits we repeat every single day with little to no thought.

When a certain activity becomes a habit for you, you no longer need grit to keep repeating it. It becomes a part of you. No matter what happens, you perform this task automatically.

Without delving too deep into the science of building habits (I describe it in more detail in my book "How to Build Self-Discipline: Resist Temptations and Reach Your Long-Term Goals"), building routines is all about two things: cues and rewards.

The cue is the signal that triggers the action you're about to perform. Reward is there to motivate you to repeat the same behavior over and over until it becomes a part of you.

For instance, writing 3,000 words is the first thing I do right after daily hygiene and exercise. I usually start writing with the first sip of tea (cue). When I finish writing, I'm free to eat, read a book or spend time pursuing my other passions (reward).

Establish similar routines for every goal you want to achieve. It doesn't necessarily have to be a routine that takes several hours to perform.

When learning a new language, it can be learning 10 new words or writing an email to a pen pal. When learning any new skill, it can be practicing it for one hour. When working to produce a specific output, it can be a specific word count, number of videos, photos, etc.

Don't Break the Chain

When famous American comic Jerry Seinfeld was still an unknown touring comic, he motivated himself to write new jokes every single day by putting a big red X over every single day he wrote[vi]. After several days, he had a short chain. It grew longer with each day. A couple of weeks later, he established a new routine with a simple motivation in his mind – he didn't want to break the long chain on his calendar.

Skipping one day makes it easier to skip the next. By putting your focus on not breaking the chain, you reduce the risk of giving up by making one, initially innocent-looking, exception.

Sometimes such simple methods are all that's needed to endure the darkest days of the dip. Even if you're in the middle of working on your goal, you can still start following this strategy and put your first big red X on your calendar today.

If you don't have a calendar, download an app on your phone or make a simple spreadsheet.

ROUTINES – THE KEY TO PERSISTENCE: QUICK RECAP

1. Set up a daily routine and follow it no matter the circumstances. Resist the temptation to keep going for longer when you have strength for it. Don't take a break when things get tough – unless you find yourself in extreme conditions. Build discipline to work on your goal every single day – with no exceptions.

2. Establish your routines on top of your existing habits. The more automated your behavior is, the less resistance you'll feel and the less likely you'll be to give up.

3. Even small actions, when you make them every single day, can produce great results in the long term. Don't disregard the power of consistent action.

4. Put a big red X on every day you stick to your goals and don't break the chain.

Chapter 3: How to Develop Mental Toughness

In sport psychology, mental toughness encompasses a wide variety of positive attributes that help a person handle difficult situations and persevere without losing confidence.

Studies[vii] suggest that mental toughness can be developed by gradual exposure to demanding situations. This simple practice teaches you how to cope and keep going when you want to give up.

Fatigue Is in Your Mind

According to a study led by exercise physiologist and marathoner Emma Ross, fatigue is all in your head[viii]. Her study on experienced runners uncovered that it's not the muscles that can't keep going on for longer during strenuous exercise – it's the brain that reduces the electrical stimulation of the working muscles.

Scientists speculate it's the brain's mechanism to prevent us from either damaging ourselves or exercising to death. You can delay this effect by slowly pushing your limits and expanding your safe zone. It's like taking your brain a little closer and closer to the edge of the cliff. Once it can look down, you take it to a higher cliff and repeat the process.

If you're working on a fitness-related goal and you're close to giving up, reminding yourself it's not your muscles that give out but your brain can help you perform one more rep. Continuous small improvements will lead to long-term progress, which in turn will ensure you won't give up on your goals too soon.

I can attribute crushing at least several of my personal records thanks to this knowledge.

Five Exercises to Become Tougher

Research conducted by Richard A. Dienstbier[ix] suggests that there are two ways to toughen up: passive toughening (intermittent exposure to stress) and active toughening (such as exercise).

Cold Exposure

One of the prime ways to toughen up is to expose yourself to cold. Studies[x] show that exposure to cold leads to rapid and intense spikes in adrenaline.

Taking cold showers or ice baths on a regular basis will lead to better coping with this stressful activity, which in turn will help you better deal with other challenging events. Swimming in cold water is even more effective (though many people couldn't think of a worse torture).

If taking a cold shower (let alone a cold bath) is too much of a challenge to you, you can also alternate between hot and cold water. 15 to 30 seconds of cold water and 15 to 30 seconds of hot water is a much more manageable way to benefit from cold exposure for people who don't cope with cold well.

Physical Activity

Exercise is another scientifically-proven way[xi] to become tougher. Whether it's running, weightlifting, swimming, or any other kind of physical activity, it helps you toughen up.

To get even more benefits from physical activity, consider pushing your limits (safely, with proper form) from time to time. Run a longer distance than usual. Lift more weight. Perform difficult exercises.

Weightlifting is particularly healthy and beneficial since it both toughens you up (especially multi-joint exercises like squats and deadlifts) and increases your strength. You can't help but feel more equipped to deal with problems in life when you shatter your personal records.

Fasting

Intermittent fasting is one of the most beneficial simple habits to both improve your health and toughen you up. Benefits of fasting are well documented, even though there are a lot of misconceptions about it[xii].

There are various ways of fasting. Some people fast for 16 hours by skipping breakfast. Others stop eating at 6 PM one day and resume eating the next day at 6 PM. People more experienced with fasting take longer breaks from eating – sometimes for up to a few days.

Start small by skipping one or two meals. Fasting may feel uncomfortable at first, but with increased practice you'll notice you no longer feel hunger like you did before.

Intermittent fasting is an inherent part of my lifestyle. Every single day, I fast for at least 16 to 20 hours, and sometimes longer. It has changed my relationship with food and helped me increase my self-control.

Note: I'm not a doctor and I don't play one in the books. Speak with your physician before you want to try cold exposure, strenuous exercise or fasting.

Meditation

Studies show[xiii] that meditation leads to improved self-control. Even five minutes spent sitting in silence, trying to focus on your breath, is enough to enjoy many health benefits of this practice[xiv].

Sitting still sounds like the easiest suggestion in this subchapter, yet most people find it extremely difficult once they try it. It's difficult to spend time in silence, trying to focus on the present moment and nothing else.

I strongly suggest meditating in the morning. You can tie it with an existing habit of brushing your teeth – meditate right after putting your toothbrush back in its place.

Do things that make you uncomfortable

Intermittent exposure to stressful situations is yet another way to improve your mental toughness. There are endless ways to deliberately make yourself uncomfortable. Here are a few things to consider:

- talking with random strangers,

- doing exercises you hate (remind yourself of your most detested moments during PE classes),

- public speaking,

- extreme sports,

- facing your other fears (fear of the dark, heights, etc.).

HOW TO DEVELOP MENTAL TOUGHNESS: QUICK RECAP

1. Fatigue is in your mind. Push yourself past your limits to train your brain not to panic under too much stress. Gradual exposure to demanding situations will help you achieve this goal.

2. Exposure to cold is one of the best ways to build mental toughness. Try cold showers or alternate hot and cold water.

3. Physical activity, and especially weightlifting, makes you a tougher and stronger person. If you want to toughen up, strenuous exercise produces the best results.

4. Fasting is another viable way to improve your mental toughness. Skip a meal or fast for a full day and learn how to control your urges.

5. Meditation improves self-control and makes you tougher by teaching you how to sit still. Even five minutes a day is enough to benefit from it.

6. Stepping outside your comfort zone by doing things you find uncomfortable is another way to build

your mental toughness. Face your fears and do awkward things to get tougher.

Chapter 4: When You're Trying Too Hard

Hard work is a success cliché that makes people work unnecessarily hard. Some of the most successful people in life achieved their goals not because of their blood, sweat, and tears, but primarily because they worked *less* than other people (but in a more focused way).

British billionaire Richard Branson is a prime example of working less and achieving more.

As he said in his interview with Inc. Magazine[xv], "Early on in your career, find someone better than yourself to run the business on a day-to-day basis. Remove yourself, maybe even from the building, and from the nitty-gritty. That way, you're going to be able to see the bigger picture and think of new areas to go into."

Branson has been following this approach since his early days. As he points out in the same interview, "In some ways it's easier today for me to oversee a few hundred companies than it was when I was hands-on running the business myself. Learning the art of delegation is absolutely key."

When you stop trying so hard, it's much easier to persevere. You no longer have to toil away with no reward and remind yourself of your goal. Things happen with much less effort, and the reward is much bigger, too.

In this chapter, we'll explore several concepts and techniques for how to follow the philosophy of "less is more" to help you keep going during hard times.

Focus on the Vital Few

The 80/20 Principle, also known as the Pareto Principle, is one of the most practical universal laws that can help you avoid many hardships and achieve more with much less work.

One of the most common reasons why people give up is because they become overwhelmed. For instance, when you start learning a new language, you've yet to become aware of how many things – grammar, vocabulary, proper pronunciation and intonation – you don't know. In psychology, it's called *unconscious incompetence*.

When you go from this phase to the second stage – *conscious incompetence* – you realize the vast deficits in your knowledge. It's during this stadium that many people give up, terrified or discouraged by how much they have to learn.

The rule of the vital few says that the minority of things matter a great deal and the majority of things don't matter a lot. The key is to focus on just a couple of crucial things and disregard the rest. Your task becomes manageable again, and you keep going with much less effort.

When you apply this rule during the stage of conscious incompetence, you'll reduce the risk of giving up.

In the case of learning languages, it's usually the ability to communicate with native speakers – basic sentences and phrases are much more important than proper grammar or getting the intonation right.

In the case of building a business, it's getting your first client, the next one, and the next one. Leave thinking about more complex business tasks for later.

In fitness, you don't have to learn more than a few basic movements (squat, deadlift, bench press, overhead press, chin-up). All the other exercises aren't necessary for most trainees.

Deconstruct each of your goals in a similar way and don't let the complexity deter you from making progress.

Disregard the Effort, Focus on the Results

The myth of hard work has instilled in many people a perverse belief that it's the effort that counts, not the results. For some strange reason, a "hard-working" person who spends 12 hours at work is a better employee than someone who works for two hours, but generates more output than the first person.

Society glorifies busyness and struggle instead of effectiveness and smart thinking.

You can observe the same phenomenon when people work on their goals. Losing weight is associated with starving, working out at the gym is associated with endless hours of extremely intensive training, and building a business is associated with sleeping four hours per night and working for the remaining 20 hours straight.

It's no wonder that people who focus on the effort burn out and give up. Switch your focus from busyness and struggle to getting results. When setting goals, always look for the easiest way to reach them.

How to Stop Operating at Suboptimal Level

All of us know how dangerous stress is to our health. Yet, the image of success people have in their minds usually means extremely hard and stressful work, frequently at the cost of stress wreaking havoc on your body.

Yet, studies suggest it's not persevering all the time that helps people operate as optimal level. In fact, taking a break can help you become more productive and prevent burnout.

If you believe that when you're under pressure you should push harder, consider the following studies.

In one study on 87 blue-collar employees in Israel,[xvi] researchers found out that – possibly unsurprisingly – vacation alleviated perceived job stress and burnout. The decline in burnout lasted for four weeks after the vacation. One break can increase your performance for an entire month.

A study conducted on eleven healthy students on the Stanford University men's varsity basketball team[xvii] found out that increased total sleep time leads to improved mood, fatigue, and vigor – all the key elements of perseverance. More sleep also increased athletic performance and reaction time.

Still unsure that working less rather than pushing more can help you keep going? Do a little experiment. For one week, record your level of dedication to your goals (a simple 1-10 scale should suffice) and maintain your current sleeping patterns. Then for the next week, sleep an hour longer than usual or take one short nap during the day and measure it again. Low energy contributes to a lot of negative thoughts and discouragement.

In an Australian study[xviii] on students during the examination period, stress led to the deterioration of diet and sleep. Students struggled with controlling their emotions, exercised less, and paid less attention to household chores and self-care habits. They also cared less about commitments and spending. How close would you be to giving up if you stopped caring about simple self-care habits?

If you can't afford sleeping longer during the night, consider taking a short nap during the day. A study on 28 air-traffic controllers in New Zealand[xix] suggests that taking a 40-minute nap at work, despite it being short and of poor quality, increases alertness and performance.

Despite overwhelming evidence that sleep and rest increase performance and willpower, so many people still believe that more is better. Yet, even the peak performers show otherwise.

Professor K. Anders Ericsson and his colleagues at Florida State University have studied top musicians, athletes, actors and chess players[xx]. The scientists found out that the elite performers typically practice in highly-focused sessions that last no more than 90 minutes. Moreover, they rarely work for more than four and a half hours a day.

As Dr. Ericsson said, "To maximize gains from long-term practice, individuals must avoid exhaustion and must limit practice to an amount from which they can completely recover on a daily or weekly basis."

All the evidence presented in these studies suggests that persistence isn't about pushing yourself to the limits. Just like Amundsen didn't push his team harder – even though they could go on longer – you will be better off sticking to working fewer hours and taking regular breaks to re-energize yourself.

Contrary to what many self-help authors suggest, persistence is more about proper rest and focus than pushing harder and harder.

WHEN YOU'RE TRYING TOO HARD: QUICK RECAP

1. The rule of the vital few says that the majority of the results come from a small part of the overall efforts. People who don't approach their goals with this principle in their minds are more likely to become overwhelmed and give up. When you focus on the essence of what you want to achieve, you'll reduce the risk of giving in.

2. Focus on the results instead of the efforts. Struggling for the sake of struggling is a sure-fire way to burn out and give up.

3. Stress and lack of proper rest will lead you to burn out. Make sure to take a break from time to time and get your mind off your goals.

4. Top performers recognize the power of proper rest and effectiveness. If the most elite athletes, musicians, actors, and chess players can succeed practicing a mere four and a half hours a day, so can you.

Chapter 5: How You Sabotage Yourself (and What to Do about It)

Even if you consider yourself a fairly persistent person, it's likely you sabotaged your goals at least several times. Self-sabotage comes in all shapes and sizes, but most frequently it starts with rationalizing why you should give up (when you shouldn't).

In this chapter, we'll explore some of the most common self-sabotage behaviors. You'll also learn how to deal with limiting beliefs that threaten your goals, sometimes without you even being aware of them.

5 Most Common Ways You Lead Yourself to Self-Sabotage

There are many causes why we sabotage ourselves, but there are five primary reasons why it happens.

Status quo bias

When you prefer the current state of affairs, you perceive any changes to the status quo as a loss[xxi]. It leads to powerful resistance to change. Even if you want to achieve your goals, you can't help but feel you're losing something. Consequently, you sabotage yourself and give up in order to return to the previous state of things.

For instance, people who want to lose weight may perceive the changes in their diet as a loss, even if eating junk food doesn't serve them.

There are two ways to deal with status quo bias in regards to giving up.

1. Remind yourself of your goals and ask yourself if the status quo serves these objectives. Let's say you want to start waking up earlier to become more productive. After a couple of days, you feel the loss of the freedom to stay up late. But does staying up late serve your goal to become more productive?

2. Ask yourself if you would pick the status quo if it hadn't already been the current state of things. If you could choose between waking up early and

staying up late, would you still choose staying up late as the optimal state of affairs?

When you become aware of the fact you want to give up because you miss the previous state of things, ask yourself the aforementioned questions. Due to loss aversion[xxii], people have a hard time losing and strongly prefer avoiding losses to acquiring gains.

In fact, studies suggest that losses hurt twice as much as gains would feel good[xxiii]. Consequently, if you want to set effective goals, the reward you'll get from them has to be at least twice as powerful as the feeling of loss you'll experience because of the sacrifices you have to make.

Restraint bias

Research shows[xxiv] that people who overestimate their ability to control impulses like hunger, drug cravings, and sexual arousal are more prone to overexpose themselves to temptations.

Due to this bias, you're likely to sabotage yourself if you believe you're great at controlling impulses.

When you're on a diet, you may be tempted to take one or two days off just because you think you're great at self-control. Unless it's a scheduled cheat day, your decision will probably lead to a permanent diet break.

If you want to write a book and set a goal to write 1,000 words a day, the restraint bias can lead you to skipping several days of writing because you believe you can always go back to your routine. The result is predictable – two weeks pass, and your routine is gone.

It's better to underestimate the power of your self-control than overestimate it. Don't expose yourself to temptations if you don't have to.

Boredom

Every time you try something new, dopamine (among others, responsible for your reward center) makes you feel good. It thrives on novelty and variation[xxv]. Advertisements prey on this phenomenon, promising you a new experience, a different taste, improved product, and so on.

The moment something becomes boring, you may become tempted to give up and seek something else. It's an extremely common pattern among entrepreneurs looking for the perfect business. Instead of focusing on just one venture, fueled by their need for variation and novelty, they jump from one idea to another. It's dopamine at work.

However, dopamine is neither good nor bad for you. It can work to your benefit as it can work to your detriment. You can benefit from the feel-good emotions it causes by introducing some variation and novelty when working on your goals.

Let's say you have a goal of losing 20 pounds and you're at the brink of giving up because your diet is bland and your exercise is boring. Why not try new (healthy) foods you have never eaten? Why not use exotic spices to bring some variation? Why not try a different sport or mix up your workouts?

When you find something that works for you, stick to it and do all in your power to keep it exciting. If it becomes too boring, the risk of self-sabotage will increase with each day.

Feeling unworthy

Low self-esteem can make you feel as if you don't deserve success. Even if things are going well, you'll sabotage yourself just because of the mistaken belief you don't deserve to achieve your goal.

Building self-esteem starts with self-awareness and self-monitoring. When you start monitoring your inner critic and replacing bad thoughts with the positive ones, you'll be on your way to kill your self-critical voice.

Making a list of your positive attributes is another useful technique to improve your self-esteem. The key is to be honest and write the list without any judgments. Once it's ready, re-read it every single day until it sinks in that you're not as worthless as you think.

Another useful method is to become kinder toward other people. When you treat other people well, they will return the favor, thus making you feel better about yourself.

In more extreme cases, such as low self-esteem caused by domestic violence, a consultation with a psychologist is the first step toward recovery. Again, I don't play a doctor.

Fear of the unknown

Even if you really want to achieve your big goals, sometimes you'll sabotage yourself just because you'll be too afraid of what's going to happen when you achieve them. It's a crippling mental block that can prevent you from achieving success in life.

One of the most effective ways to overcome the fear of the unknown is to speak with people who have achieved your goal. The more you understand the process – and what reaching the goal entails – the less afraid you'll be of achieving your goal.

Each time you achieve a small win, look back and ask yourself if it's scary to be on the other side. Gradual changes will make you realize your life won't dramatically change overnight.

Fear of the unknown is often related to the fear of losing control. Some people sabotage themselves when they think something is too good to last just to maintain their belief they're in control.

Deal with this problem by gradually letting go of control over the small things. The more often you expose yourself to situations where you have little to no control, the more at peace you'll be with the feeling of uncertainty.

How to Overcome Limiting Beliefs

Limiting beliefs are yet another reason why people sabotage themselves. They're so important, they deserve their own subchapter.

Limiting beliefs don't get a lot of publicity in your head. They work behind the scenes, leading you to make the wrong choices and give up for the wrong reasons. Some of the most common limiting beliefs (and their results) include:

- *I need to drive myself to exhaustion to succeed* – if you believe you can't achieve success without working 12 hours a day, sooner or later you'll drive yourself to burnout and give up due to the lack of energy.

- *I failed so many times it will happen again* – experiencing failures can make some people enter a vicious cycle. Even if they set new goals and work on them, sooner or later they remember their past failures and let them influence their current behavior.

- *It's not possible* – comes in many flavors, but always comes down to the feeling of doubt. How are you supposed to persevere if you don't believe it's possible?

- *It's too late to change* – usually the result of comparing yourself to other people who achieved something sooner than you. You give up just because you believe you have to achieve something before some arbitrary time (e.g., you may believe you're too old to start a business if you're fifty).

- *I have no idea how to do it* – you assume you're much less intelligent than you are. As a result, you give up at the first sign of problems or things you have to learn.

There are various ways to reverse limiting beliefs. The most helpful way to overcome them is to look for evidence you're wrong.

For instance, let's assume I believe that if I don't have a lot of free time during the day, I might as well give up now, as I will never build a business. To reverse this belief, I would look for people who have built a successful business despite numerous responsibilities in their lives.

If there are such people, I have proof my belief is wrong.

Then I would ask myself how I can replicate their results and if my new belief ("I can build a successful business by working on it two hours per day") would serve me better.

My limiting belief won't magically disappear overnight, but each time I deconstruct it this way, it will weaken – soon to be replaced with an enabling belief.

Each time the old limiting belief appears in your mind, remind yourself why it's wrong. If possible, reach out to people who achieved your goal and ask them for advice on how to push through.

You can use a similar framework for every limiting belief you have. The key is to stop identifying yourself with the belief and question it. By successfully reversing each limiting belief that would otherwise lead you to giving up, you'll experience dramatic personal growth and become more persistent than ever before.

HOW YOU SABOTAGE YOURSELF (AND WHAT TO DO ABOUT IT): QUICK RECAP

1. Status quo bias will tempt you to return to the previous state of things. Battle it by asking yourself if the status quo serves these objectives. Would you still have chosen the status quo if it hadn't already been in place?

2. Make sure the gains you'll experience from your goal are at least twice as good as the losses you're going to suffer.

3. The restraint bias will lead you to thinking you're better at self-control than you really are. Don't overexpose yourself to temptations. Underestimate your ability to control your impulses rather than the other way around.

4. Introduce novelty and variation when working on your goals to avoid boredom that will lead to burnout.

5. Work on your self-esteem to avoid sabotaging yourself because you do not feel worthy of the reward. The top ways to build self-esteem include

monitoring your thoughts, acknowledging your strengths and being kinder to others.

6. Research what will happen when you achieve your goal to reduce your risk of the unknown. Practice letting go of control to become more at peace with the feeling of uncertainty.

7. Limiting beliefs can lead you to self-sabotage. Eliminate them by coming up with the evidence against them.

Chapter 6: How to Develop Psychological Resilience

Psychological resilience is the ability to adapt to stress and adversity, two reasons why many people give up before they achieve their goals.

Which personality traits affect psychological resilience? What are the top techniques to become more resilient? In this chapter you'll find the answer to these questions.

The Most Important Personality Trait of Gritty People

Studies[xxvi] show that grit is strongly associated with conscientiousness. People who are conscientious are thorough, careful, vigilant, organized, efficient, industrious, and self-controlled. They are usually reliable and systematic. When taken to the extreme, they are perfectionists and/or workaholics.

If conscientiousness isn't your strong suit, don't despair. There are several ways to become more conscientious.

1. Focus on improving specific aspects of conscientiousness. For instance, create a habit to organize your desk and clean it every week, or focus on being punctual.

2. Make daily plans. Organize your life by setting plans and sticking to them. You can carry a small notepad with you (or use an app on your phone). This will improve your self-discipline, which will in turn make you more persistent.

3. Use technology to remind yourself of important things. If you have a bad case of forgetting about things to do, set reminders on your phone or computer.

4. Keep your word. If you promise someone something, no matter how small it is, do it. People will think of you as a reliable person, which in turn will make you better at sticking to the promises you make to yourself.

5. Consider de-cluttering. Read about minimalism – the philosophy of "less is more" that suggests owning fewer things and focusing more on the

experiences. It will make your surroundings less chaotic, which in turn will make you more organized.

The Most Important Skill to Build Resilience

Scientists define psychological resilience as "flexibility in response to changing situational demands, and the ability to bounce back from negative emotional experiences.[xxvii]" People who are resilient experience positive emotions even during stressful events, which helps them quickly rebound despite adversity.

Consequently, the most important skill to build resilience is to learn how to turn your struggles into something positive. The primary technique of doing this is *reframing*.

Reframing is a way of turning bad experiences and concepts into more positive ones. Instead of thinking about your problems as something that prevents you from achieving your goal, you can turn them into opportunities to grow.

When you're struggling to keep going, you can reframe your struggles as a part of an incredible story you'll tell when you achieve your goal.

You can combine this technique with visualization. Imagine the day you've achieved your goal and remind yourself of all your struggles and the obstacles you had to overcome. When you go back to the present moment, you'll see your problems from a new, more empowering perspective. This will build your resilience.

Here are a couple of examples of reframing.

An entrepreneur who has five failed projects behind her realizes each of her previous businesses wasn't in fact a failure – it was an opportunity to learn what doesn't work. Consequently, each new project can only be better.

A person who's trying to lose weight couldn't resist the cravings and gorged on junk food for several days in a row. She can think of her failure as an opportunity to find out what makes her lose control.

A salesperson who wants to become the most effective employee in the company faces rejection after rejection. Each rejection makes her deal better with rejection, which promises a great career in sales (and a great motivational story to tell when she becomes a sales manager).

Five More Ways to Build Resilience

Some people are naturally equipped to deal with adversity, while others have to develop this skill. There are five primary ways of building resilience.

Embrace change

Flexibility is one of the most important aspects of resilience. People who have a hard time adapting to different situations – adverse or not – struggle with sticking to their goals when they're forced to change their approach.

While regular people find abrupt, big changes overwhelming, resilient individuals use these events to learn from them. Instead of despairing, they adapt and thrive.

The ability to embrace change comes with practice. Frequent changes in your life – both just small changes of your habits or big career changes – can help you build this skill and become more flexible.

Consider setting up regular experiments in your life and shaking up your routine this way.

If you always wake up at eight, try waking up at six and adapt to it. If you always eat five meals per day, try eating one meal per day. Pick different routes to work each day or work in a different place if you're self-employed.

Traveling to foreign countries, and especially the explorative kind of travel (not just tanning at the swimming pool), is another powerful way to become more adaptive to changes. The more different the culture of the country you're visiting, the more you'll learn how to adapt to changes.

Develop a strong network of supportive friends and family

Resilient people, no matter how well-equipped to deal with adversity, don't go it alone. A strong social network is a must if you're working on big goals that are guaranteed to throw at you numerous larger-than-life challenges.

The knowledge that you can always fall back on your supportive circle of friends and family members will help you stay calm during the stressful events.

Be optimistic

Optimism and resilience go hand in hand. People who are resilient are able to see the positives even in the direst of circumstances. The most important skill to become more optimistic is reframing, which we already discussed. Below are three more ways to bring more optimism in your life.

1. Smile. Studies[xxviii] show that people who are unable to frown because of Botox injections experience a significantly less negative mood than people who can frown. You can do it the natural way, though – smile more, even if you don't necessarily feel like doing so. Putting on a fake smile will still improve your mood.

2. Count your blessings. Various[xxix] studies[xxx] show that expressing gratitude boosts your mood, increases long-term happiness and decreases

depressive symptoms. A simple daily practice of noting down three things you're thankful for is enough to experience the beneficial effects of gratitude.

3. Follow the ABCDE model. Psychologist Albert Ellis created the initial ABC model of adversity, belief, and consequence. Martin Seligman, one of the most renowned psychologists known for his research of positive psychology[xxxi], added D – disputation, and E – energization, to this model.

Adversity – describe a recent adversity as an objective statement.

Belief – record what you were saying to yourself when faced with the adversity.

Consequences – what did you feel or what did you do because of it?

Disputation – find evidence against your belief or put it into a different perspective.

Energization – how did you feel when you disputed your belief?

Here's how it works on a real-life example:

Adversity – *I applied for a new job and got rejected.*

Belief – *I'm just not good enough. I'll never get a better job.*

Consequences – *I feel worthless. I stop looking for a new job and feel sorry for myself. Consequently, I feel even worse than before.*

Disputation – *That's not true because I worked at X a couple of years ago and they always praised me.*

OR

Maybe it just wasn't the right job for me. The fact that they rejected me doesn't mean I'm not good enough. There are many more companies I haven't applied to yet.

Energization – *I feel much more confident in my abilities to find a new job. I know I can bring a lot to the table and will show it to my next potential employer.*

Use the same model to change your default responses to more positive ones.

Take care of yourself

A common reaction to adversity when you don't possess a lot of resilience is to stop taking care of yourself. You ignore eating healthy, exercise, sleeping well, and you stop doing things which make you happy.

Resilient people don't change their habits when they face a crisis. Even when you're experiencing powerful setbacks, you can still take care of your needs.

Make sure to nurture yourself at all times – in both good and bad circumstances. If your default behavior when faced with a crisis is to neglect your needs, force yourself to stick to your habits – even if you don't feel particularly happy about it.

Develop your problem-solving skills

The knowledge that you're able to deal even with the most complex problems thrown your way will make you a more resilient person. And this knowledge only comes from the ability to solve problems and real-world experience.

Whenever you're faced with a problem, come up with a list of ways to handle it. The more often you exercise your idea muscle, the more skilled you'll become at solving problems.

Practice every chance you get. Listen to your friends and help them solve their problems. Come up with hypothetic challenges and come up with ideas for how to handle them. Look at every problem from different perspectives. Don't be afraid to solve it in an unconventional way.

HOW TO DEVELOP PSYCHOLOGICAL RESILIENCE: QUICK RECAP

1. Conscientiousness is the most important trait of gritty people. To become a more conscientious person, make yourself more organized and reliable. Consider following the philosophy of minimalism to reduce the chaos around you.

2. Use reframing to become more resilient. Each time you're dealing with a bad situation, find the positives in it.

3. Make small and big changes in your life to become more flexible and become better at embracing change.

4. Develop a strong social circle to support you on your journey to reach your goals.

6. Optimism will help you become more resilient. Start with smiling more, as even a fake smile will improve your mood. Express gratitude on a daily basis. Follow the ABCDE model (adversity, belief, consequence, disputation, energization) to exhibit a more positive attitude on a daily basis.

7. Nurture yourself at all times. Don't let a crisis turn you into a wreck because it will make you even less equipped to deal with the problem.

8. Practice your problem-solving skills to increase your confidence. Come up with solutions to the problems you have, the problems of your friends and hypothetic problems.

Chapter 7: Five Techniques to Be Relentless

Even the most persistent people sometimes battle with doubt and are tempted to give up. Fortunately, there are several effective techniques you can use to greatly reduce the temptation to give up.

Use the first two techniques before you set a goal. The remaining three techniques will help you when you're struggling.

Set Stakes

Studies show that commitment contracts are effective as a tool for helping people save money[xxxii]. You can set stakes for virtually every other goal and achieve similar results.

The more is at stake if you give up, the less tempted you'll be to throw in the towel. If you want to ensure success, set the stakes before you start working on your goal.

For instance, if you want to start waking up earlier, give your early-rising roommate a check for $50 and let her cash it if you don't wake up at a specified hour.

If you want to lose weight, penalize yourself $50 for every cupcake you eat when you're dieting. It won't take long to give up on your favorite unhealthy foods if they're going to cost you 50 times more than usual.

Negative motivation can work wonders when positive motivation isn't enough to keep you going.

Setting stakes is also a perfect way to assess how badly you want to achieve your goal. If you're reluctant to set stakes, chances are you're afraid you'll give up. If that's the case, then it's extremely unlikely you'll achieve your goal without proper negative motivation.

StickK.com is the biggest online community for people interested in setting stakes to reach their goals.

Get Yourself Accountable

Public accountability is a variation of setting financial stakes. Instead of making yourself pay for giving up, you'll risk public shaming. For some people, this technique produces a much more motivating effect than the prospect of losing money.

One of the easiest ways to get yourself accountable is to partner up with another person who wants to achieve a similar goal. When two people keep each other accountable, they're both much more likely to achieve their goals than when they do it alone.

Studies show that exercising with a partner improves performance on aerobic exercises[xxxiii]. Moreover, research suggests that working out with a slightly better partner will make you more persistent[xxxiv].

You can also tell your goal to all your friends and family (or just share it on social media). It's much harder to give up if you know you'll disappoint people close to you – especially if you're working on a goal that would benefit them, too.

Another way to get yourself accountable is to work with an experienced coach. Professional guidance will increase your confidence and offer you powerful support that will help you keep going when you encounter obstacles.

Re-Read Your Vision

And if you don't have one, write it.

A vision is a document that describes how you picture your life in a given timeframe (say, one year). However, you don't necessarily have to write a vision describing every little aspect of your life (although it's a powerful motivator, too). You can write a short vision describing the achievement of a single goal. Use images and videos to make your vision stronger and more appealing.

For instance, if you want to lose weight and become fitter, find a picture of a person who looks the way you'd like to look. Describe how you feel, how strong you are, and how often you exercise.

If you want to build a successful business, find images of things or experiences you'll buy with the money your business will generate. Write down the vision of how your business serves its clients, how your employees feel about it, and how you feel as the owner.

If you want to get a new job, make a list of your dream employers. Find pictures of their offices and other images that will motivate you to keep looking for a new job.

Ask Yourself Focusing Questions

It's easy to lose focus on your goal when you experience bad emotions and feel like it makes no sense to go on longer. Before you make the final decision, ask yourself several questions:

1. Would you be happy if you gave up and your life remained the same?

Sometimes all it takes to keep going is to remind yourself of the end goal.

2. What's the worst that can happen if you keep going and don't achieve your goal?

Arnold Schwarzenegger once said, "Strength does not come from winning. Your struggles develop your strengths. When you go through hardships and decide not to surrender, that is strength."

Even if you don't achieve your goal, the person you had to become when striving to reach it was probably more than worth it.

3. How would it feel to tell other people why you gave up?

Would you feel happy to tell your friend you gave up because you prefer watching TV to becoming a fit person? Would you like telling your spouse you stopped trying to quit smoking because the feeling a cigarette gives you is more important than spending more years with her?

4. How many sacrifices have you made?

Loss aversion can make you pursue the wrong goals, but you can also use it to motivate yourself to keep going when you know you're working on the right thing. When you think about all the time, money, and effort you invested in striving for your goal, you'll be much less likely to walk away.

5. What would you tell your closest friend if you traded places with her?

Look at your struggles from a different perspective. It will give you a fresh point of view and help you focus on the big picture.

What if it was your friend who wanted to lose weight? Would you tell her to give up because she misses cupcakes too much or would you help her and tell her she's doing great?

What would you tell a friend who's working on growing his business, but clients don't come knocking? Would you tell him to throw in the towel or motivate him to try new marketing techniques?

Talk to Yourself

Sport psychology research[xxxv] confirms the beneficial effect of self-talk on performance. Athletes usually use it to improve their technique and focus, but self-talk also works outside of sports. You can use it to improve your focus on the task at hand or to motivate yourself when you're struggling.

If you're working on your business and you have to call several potential clients, you can use self-talk to prepare yourself for the next conversation. It can be a short phrase ("smile") or a longer motivational sentence ("I'm calm, professional and convincing").

If you're working on a fitness-related goal, a simple "keep going," "you can make it," or "you're stronger than you think" can help you squeeze a bit more out of your body.

Giving yourself a pep talk, as corny as it can sometimes feel, can provide you with a short-term boost of motivation.

FIVE TECHNIQUES TO BE RELENTLESS: QUICK RECAP

1. Use the power of negative motivation to reduce the temptation to give up. The most powerful ways to benefit from negative motivation are setting stakes and public accountability. The perspective of losing a considerable amount of money or public shaming can do wonders to your ability to persevere.

2. When you're struggling, motivate yourself to keep going by reading your vision. If you don't have it, write it. Make it a detailed description of your end goal.

3. Ask yourself focusing questions to prevent giving up for the wrong reason. Would you be happy if you gave up and your life remained the same? What's the worst that can happen if you keep going and don't achieve your goal? How would it feel to tell other people why you gave up? How many sacrifices have you made? What would you tell your closest friend if you traded places with her?

4. Use self-talk to get a short-term boost of motivation.

Chapter 8: Seven Common Mistakes to Avoid

In this chapter, we'll discuss some of the most common mistakes you should avoid if you want to stick to your goals and keep going – even in spite of difficulties.

Unrealistic Expectations

Due to the phenomenon known as the false hope syndrome[xxxvi], some people set unrealistic expectations and keep repeating the same mistake over and over again.

People who fall victim to the false hope syndrome (and it's more common than you think) make frequent attempts to change themselves. They give up when they realize they will never achieve their goal as quickly or as easily as they initially assumed.

In order to avoid this behavior, always research the average results people get when setting a specific goal.

For instance, if you want to go on a diet, learn how much you can expect to lose per week instead of assuming you can lose 10 pounds every single week. If you want to build a business, read articles written by seasoned entrepreneurs to find out how long it takes an inexperienced person to build a successful business. If you want to learn a new skill, research what you can expect to master in a month, three months or any other timeframe.

Such simple research will prepare you for the real world, which often differs a lot from the unrealistic expectations of beginners who are yet to become aware of how hard something is.

Focusing on the Event Instead of the Process

Self-help literature suggests that the best way to motivate yourself to work on your goal is to imagine it in great detail. Yet, there's more to it than just visualizing your success.

An experiment[xxxvii] conducted by UCLA researchers has shown that college freshmen who visualized good study habits experienced less anxiety and better outcomes than students who visualized getting a good grade.

Another similar study[xxxviii] suggests that people who spend time thinking about how to implement a plan to achieve a specific goal perform better and feel more optimistic about it than people who think about the potential reward.

When you spend more time thinking and implementing your plans rather than fantasizing about the potential reward, you'll be more likely to stick to your goals.

It doesn't mean there's no place for good old visualization – sometimes imagining future success can enhance your motivation and keep you going. It can also help you spot mistakes and improve your performance.

A technique called visual motor behavior rehearsal[xxxix] is one of the most fundamental techniques in sport psychology. The first step is to close your eyes and relax. Then, you visualize an aspect of your performance (or your success) from start to finish. Such regular practice is both motivational and offers useful feedback to improve your results.

A study by Noelia A. Vasquez and Roger Buehler[xl] suggests that visualizing your success from the third-person point of view is better than doing it from the first-person perspective.

According to the researchers, when you imagine yourself in the third-person, it helps you highlight the larger meaning and significance of your goal – which leads to a more powerful motivational impact.

Try both approaches to find out which one works better for you.

Listening to People with Limiting Beliefs

Limiting beliefs can come not only from within you, but also from other people. Negative social influence can sometimes break your goals, even if you're otherwise a persistent person.

Each time someone remarks you won't achieve a certain goal, ask yourself whether what she's saying comes from her limiting beliefs or from a valid point of view. It's quite easy to discern between opinions and facts when you ask people for evidence to back their claims. If they can't provide it, they're voicing their opinions – which you should (usually) disregard.

Many successful people, such as Jim Rohn, Tony Robbins or Richard Branson, praise the importance of the empowering social circle. When you're surrounded by individuals who support your goals and work on their own goals, you're much more likely to transform your life. Hanging out with pessimistic and lazy people will lead to the total opposite.

Making Rash Decisions

Making important decisions without taking at least several days to give yourself time to think about them is a sure-fire way to make the wrong decision.

Oftentimes, people who give up when the going gets tough give up only because the short-term pain influenced them to such an extent they decided to give up instinctively ("it hurts so much I have to stop").

Pause and reflect before you make an important decision. Come up with a set of decision-making rules. For instance:

- I never make an important decision when I'm tired.

- I never make an important decision when I'm influenced by a negative emotion (sadness, anger, frustration).

- I never make an important decision on a whim. I always give myself 24 hours to change my mind.

Most successful investors use systems that take their emotions out of the equation. Thanks to this simple rule, they don't make rash decisions that would ruin their finances.

Discounting Slow Progress

Slow progress is still progress, yet some people consider it a viable reason to give up. Unless you absolutely have to achieve something in a given timeframe and know it's impossible, giving up just because your progress is slow is a mistake.

Tweak what you're doing and find ways to increase your progress rate instead of giving up. Even if you can't find a way to go faster, sticking to your goal is still a better choice than giving up. In the first case, you'll eventually achieve your goal. In the second case, the only guarantee is that everything will stay the same.

Some people give up because they don't see progress at all. It's easy to overlook small progress, especially when you're working on a big goal.

To avoid making such a mistake, quantify your progress as much as possible. Track your abilities and performance. For instance, if you're learning a new language, you can periodically complete online tests to assess your skills.

Letting the Past Define You

Past failures shouldn't affect what you're doing now, yet many of us are susceptible to brooding on the things that didn't go well. Such negative thinking can affect your thinking when you're struggling and make you believe you're bound to repeat your old mistakes.

How do you deal with this problem and escape the vicious cycle? You shift your focus from the past to the present moment and consider each goal a fresh start. The past has power over you because you let it affect your thinking. When you let these thoughts go (and it takes self-monitoring to make it happen), you'll reduce the risk of entering the vicious cycle again.

Whining and Letting Others Complain around You

Complaining about the lack of results is a sure-fire way to lose motivation and give up. If you want to reduce the number of negative thoughts in your mind, consider trying an experiment created by bestselling author Will Bowen – go without complaining for 21 days in a row[xli].

The negative effect of complaining on your success doesn't stop with you, though.

In his book "Three Simple Steps: A Map to Success in Business and Life,"[xlii] bestselling author Trevor Blake cites research conducted on the hippocampus by Robert Sapolsky at Stanford University's School of Medicine. The Hippocampus is a part of the brain that is highly sensitive to negative stimuli.

Sapolsky found that exposure to stressors – such as listening to someone whining or gossiping –

elevates cortisol levels. It hampers synaptic connections and speeds up cell death, thus making the hippocampus shrink. As a result, the hippocampus, as Blake writes, "declines in cognitive function, including the ability to retain information and adapt to new situations."

In other words, when you let others complain around you, you not only feel unnecessary stress, but also become dumber with time. And as we already discussed, the ability to adapt to new situations is the most important skill for resilience.

Sapolsky suggests four ways to deal with this problem[xliii]:

1. Monitor your thoughts. Each time you complain, turn it into a positive thought.

2. Avoid negative people. Each time you find yourself in a negative conversation, escape it.

3. Ignore complainers if you can't avoid them. Fill your mind with positive thoughts while they complain around you.

4. Tell people to come up with solutions. When someone complains to you, ask her what she intends

to do about it. Oftentimes, it will stop the complainer from whining around you.

SEVEN COMMON MISTAKES TO AVOID: QUICK RECAP

1. Do some research before you set a goal. Unrealistic expectations are one of the most common reasons why people give up.

2. Focus on the process instead of the event. Get a boost of motivation by visualizing the reward, but also make sure to spend ample time visualizing the process. It will prepare you to deal better with challenges and make the goal appear more attainable.

3. Avoid people with limiting beliefs. A self-limiting opinion of your friend can decrease your motivation just as effectively as your own limiting beliefs.

4. People often give up on a whim when they can't endure the short-term pain associated with working on their goal. Give yourself time before you make any important decisions and remind yourself that this too shall pass.

5. Slow progress is not a good reason to give up. When something works – even if it works slowly – focus on tweaking it to make it work better.

6. Let go of any thoughts of the past influencing the present moment. People give up too frequently simply because they let their past failures define their present and future.

7. Monitor your negative thoughts and get rid of them. Try to go 21 days in a row without complaining. Remember that surrounding yourself with people with a negative attitude poisons your mind and makes you dumber. Three ways to deal with habitual whiners include: avoiding them, ignoring them and filling your mind with positive thoughts, and asking people what they intend to do to solve their problems.

Chapter 9: Six Experts Share Their Top Techniques to Never Give Up

To share with you a different perspective on persistence, I invited six experts – authors and bloggers – to share their thoughts about this topic. Below are their answers.

Stephen Guise, Bestselling Author of "Mini Habits: Smaller Habits, Bigger Results"

On my way to becoming an internationally-best-selling author with my first book, which is now being translated into a dozen languages, one might think I'm an overnight success. But truly, I nearly quit my blog – the one I needed to launch this book – six separate times! It was persistence that brought me to where I am, and there were two key things that helped me keep going.

First, I didn't start the blog because I wanted to make money. I started the blog because I enjoyed analyzing life through words, and wanted to share my ideas with more than just family and friends. When I didn't get a lot of attention for the first couple of years, I remembered that I didn't write because I wanted money or fame. This detached my work from results, which allowed me to continue.

Second, I believed in what I was doing. If you don't believe in what you're doing, persistence is going to be nearly impossible. Self-belief in general or in a particular area comes with practice. I had been writing for a year before I considered quitting the first time, and I had developed into a better writer in that time. Seeing that improvement also helped me to keep going.

To summarize, persist by first connecting your pursuit to a genuine interest that's not driven by superficial things like money or fame. This interest can drive you to the point where you'll see progress and improvement. Then, you'll see progress and develop a self-belief that if you can't do it now, you'll get there soon.

Buy Stephen's book Mini Habits here:

http://www.amazon.com/dp/B00HGKNBDK

Joel Runyon, Blogger at ImpossibleHQ.com

You need one thing. One thing to hold onto. One amazingly rock-solid reason for doing what you're doing. You need to have a bulletproof answer to the question, "Why am I doing this?" Because when your lungs are screaming, your body is tired, your brain is fried and every ounce of your being wants to quit – you need to be able to come back to that one thing, and let it be what makes you take the next step.

Read Joel's blog at: http://www.impossiblehq.com

Serena Star-Leonard, Bestselling Author of "How to Retire in 12 Months: Turning Passion into Profit"

There are many reasons why you may give up on something. If you have genuinely lost interest, or perhaps never had it in the first place, giving up may be inevitable. But if you are tempted to give up because things got really hard or you are facing seemingly insurmountable challenges, here are my tips for pushing through.

1. Stop and breathe. When you are really close to your project, you can get a skewed perspective on reality, especially if things appear to be crumbling or out of control. I find it helps to remove myself completely for a period of time.

If you are very involved, take a couple of days off and do something completely different. Do something that usually fills you up and gives you great peace, joy or calm. Sometimes just the act of leaving something that seems so important can give you some perspective. Stop, breathe, sleep on it, catch up with friends and you will often find the solution you need falls into place – and often you will realise that it wasn't such a hard problem after all.

2. Brainstorm ways you can do things differently. If you are really thinking about giving up on your goal, sit down, and write a list of 10 or 20 ways you could do things differently that will increase your chances of success.

Be super creative and let yourself come up with plausible and perhaps even seemingly implausible ways you could change how you approach your goal each day. We often bash our heads against the wall because a routine or strategy that is simply not working. Give yourself creative licence to change it up and see what you can come up with.

3. Remember that everything can change overnight. Even if you have had no joy for six months or two years in your project, you have to remember that everything can change overnight.

Imagine that tomorrow you had some great breakthrough in your project. What actions could you take to make that breakthrough a reality? Who could you call? What could you offer? What can you create? What action will you take? Who are you avoiding approaching? The answers to those questions should create a set of possible actions that could alter your results... fast!

Check Serena's site here: http://in12months.com/

Derek Doepker, Bestselling Author of "Why You're Stuck"

Three Magic Words to Stick to Any Resolution

Do you ever get started with something feeling like you can take on the world, and then "life" gets in the way to throw you off track?

There's one technique that's a bit of a "secret weapon" of mine for staying on track no matter how challenging things get. I call it my "three magic words" technique.

I simply ask myself, "Can I just...?" and then insert an action so easy I can do it no matter how unmotivated I feel.

Let's say I don't feel like doing an hour-long workout. I can ask, "Can I just do the warmup?" If even that's too overwhelming, I'll ask, "Can I just do the first 30 seconds?" After that I'd ask, "Can I just do a little more? One more rep? One more exercise?" I can always stop once I've reached a point where I've felt like I've done all I can and still feel a sense of accomplishment.

Have you ever noticed that it's *after* you start doing something, *then* you feel like you want to keep on going?

Instead of trying to get motivation, try to get momentum. The motivation will naturally follow.

Success breeds success. Each time you're victorious at doing even a little thing, your sense of accomplishment and desire to do more will grow.

This means any time you feel like quitting, give yourself just the tiniest step in the right direction, ideally something that takes you less than a minute to do. Then if that's all you can do for that day, then great! Reward yourself by saying, "I did *something* when I felt like quitting and that makes me awesome!"

With this self-reward process, every single time you follow through is critical to making a habit stick. If your rewards are far off down the road, you'll rarely feel good enough in the short-term to stick with your resolution. This means the whole, "Yeah... well I *should have* done more. I'm pathetic!" type of self-talk has to go. Changing your inner dialogue is an often overlooked part of this whole process.

Reward yourself every single time you follow through on even the tiniest step in the right direction. This feeling of accomplishment will push you to do even more.

This method always works so long as you make sure you give yourself an easy target to shoot for. Even if it takes months to build momentum, using these three magic words, "Can I just," to find the smallest step you're willing to take is guaranteed to take you farther than doing nothing at all.

Derek Doepker shows people how to create better habits in 5 minutes a day in his book "The Healthy Habit Revolution."

He is also the author of the #1 best-selling personal development book "Why You're Stuck" and founder of the blog Excuse Proof Fitness. You can connect with him at http://facebook.com/derekdoepker

Michal Stawicki, Bestselling Author of the "Trickle-Down Mindset: The Missing Element in Your Personal Success"

An ounce of prevention is worth a pound of cure.

What to do when you feel like quitting? Well, if you feel like quitting it's about a few months too late to do anything. It means that you don't believe in what you're doing. It doesn't excite you. You don't feel it's worth your time and effort. Something went wrong a long time ago.

The reason for this feeling is rarely sensible. I can come up with only two instances when it's justified: it doesn't provide the results you want or you're exhausted and have no strength to finish your task. Both of these sensible reasons demand sensible solutions. Firstly, tweak your actions so you'll start getting desirable effects. Secondly, change your lifestyle, so you'll have higher energy levels on a daily basis.

To ensure results, you should consider more than just your current level of motivation. You need a plan, metrics, and a tracking system. Some external validation is also not a bad idea (a mentor, a coach, a like-minded community of people, a mastermind group or an accountability partner). You should develop your plan and start tracking your results from the start.

To improve your energy levels, you need to examine yourself. What do you eat? How often do you exercise? How long do you sleep? Then you need to amend your daily routines to improve your performance. You're exhausted because of your lifestyle, not of the job at hand. If you lack strength, my best guess is that you're sleep deprived.

The best trick for that is to take a brief nap. A power nap can bring you back to "almost normal" faster and without the side effects of stimulants.

Let's analyze what lies behind the "I feel like quitting" statement. First of all, it's a feeling – something short-term and counter to rationality.

The first sign of this feeling is your self-talk. Here are some things I say when I try to discourage myself from action: "And what's that for? Nobody really appreciates your job anyway," "I've slogged for too long. I deserve some rest," "Take it easy, it's not so important, is it?" "This is hard, I need some rest; turn on the movie and forget about the world for the next two hours."

All those statements are expressions of feelings lurking behind them, a hunger for acceptance, a desire for relaxation and comfort, or boredom. The best immediate solution is to amend your self-dialog.

It's not hard to outtalk your emotions; they are dumb and you are smart. But noticing your discouraging self-talk and fighting it isn't easy. You need some practice. It's all about prevention again. I recommend journaling and/or meditation to increase your awareness of your self-talk.

Usually the rationalizations behind your emotions are not only dumb, but are also false. In my case "nobody really appreciates your job anyway" simply means that my wife hasn't praised me lately. It's her acceptance I'm striving for the most.

The easiest counterargument to your self-whining is: "Is it true?"

Does nobody appreciate me? Of course somebody does. I have many testimonials from my readers saying that my work is valuable. Do I deserve rest? Of course not. Rest is not something you need to earn. It's a necessary part of life. Do I need to rest right now? That's a valid question. Is what I'm doing unimportant? If yes, then I should definitely do something else instead.

Asking yourself, "Is it true?" leads to feeble answers from your subconscious mind. These answers can be easily dismantled by further questioning. For example:

"This is hard. I need some rest."

"Is it true?"

"Yes, I'm tired."

"What was so tiresome?"

"Ohhh... well... yeah... I slept for just 7 hours... and I've already been working two hours!"

And now you know that you're just making excuses.

In my experience this feeling is the result of neglecting the foundations, especially your personal philosophy. Personal philosophy is the attitude you adopt for the conduct of your life. It's the conglomerate of your beliefs. It serves as the filtering mechanism for all ideas bombarding your mind.

I recommend prevention. Don't worry about the current lack of motivation. Work on the constant flow of motivation and this feeling will never show up or will be nipped in the bud. A long time ago, my subconscious gave up any direct attempts to discourage me from action. As a part of my personal philosophy, I adopted the belief: "If I quit, I will never know the results." Quitting is simply not an option in my worldview.

Shifting your own beliefs is not an easy job. It may be done relatively quickly, but you need to be a master of NLP (Neuro-linguistic programming) to achieve lasting results in a short time-span. Most of us aren't, and thus I recommend a more balanced approach: change your data sources, change the people you interact with and change your self-talk.

If you change these three elements alone, you will change your life forever. No magic, no woo-woo involved. Opening up to new information, new people and improving your internal dialog will cause the natural process of "belief osmosis" to work.

I challenge you to consume just one new medium (blog, podcast, etc.), join just one new group of people, and meditate or journal for five minutes a day. Do it for 100 days and try to remain the same person.

You will prevent yourself from quitting instead of expending a lot of energy to fight the temptation when it comes.

Michal is a bestselling self-help author (you can check his books here: www.amazon.com/author/michalstawicki) and blogger at http://www.expandbeyondyourself.com/

Hung Pham, Bestselling Author of "Break Through: 12 Powerful Steps to Destroy Your Mental Barriers and Achieve Success"

For the better part of my 20s I suffered from depression, addiction, and was drowning in debt. There were many days where not only did I feel like giving up, but I wouldn't mind if a car crashed into me and took my life. I just felt like I was such a waste of a life. Looking back now, it's very sad that I would think that way but during that time I couldn't help it.

I'm happy to say that I'm in a much better place now, out of debt, recovered from addiction, and more importantly, I'm thriving as an entrepreneur. The best pieces of advice that I can give to anyone who feels like giving up are the following:

1. If you are suffering from depression or addiction, seek help right away. For most of my 20s I was embarrassed to seek help and thought I could beat it on my own, but in reality, you need to seek help as a start.

2. If you want to give up because your goals seem insurmountable, look for the small wins. When I was trying to get out of $60,000 worth of debt, I started small. I tried to work backwards to figure out a system that would allow me to pay off my debt within a reasonable time. It's important to look for the small wins because those add up to the bigger wins.

3. If you find yourself stretched too thin because you have so much going on in your life, re-prioritize

what is most important. Cut out all the B.S. For me, it was about getting better and mentally healthier. Once I did that, all of the other aspects of my life, such as my career and business, began to thrive.

4. And lastly, if you just don't have the confidence anymore, remember this: nothing hard ever came easy to anyone. Life is supposed to be hard and for those of us who really want to make an impact, there's always a struggle. But the value is in the journey and not the destination. I never sought to be an entrepreneur, but in the process of getting better I realized how much I can help others through my experience. That's the one thought that stays with me every day.

All the things you want in life are outside of your comfort zone.

Hung is a bestselling self-help author whose books you can check here: http://amazon.com/author/hungpham. Sign up for his newsletter for more tips: http://www.missionandpossible.com/

SIX EXPERTS SHARE THEIR TOP TECHNIQUES TO NEVER GIVE UP: QUICK RECAP

Stephen Guise:

1. Have a different motivation than external goals like money or fame.

2. Have a belief in what you're doing.

Joel Runyon:

1. Have a bulletproof answer to the question, "Why am I doing this?"

Serena Star-Leonard:

1. Leave your problems for a couple of days to gain a fresh perspective.

2. Brainstorm 10 to 20 ways to do things differently and increase your chances of success.

3. Imagine you had a breakthrough in your project and ask yourself what could help you make it a reality.

Derek Doepker:

1. Instead of trying to get motivation, try to get momentum. Ask yourself, "Can I just...?" and come up with a small action you can do no matter how unmotivated you are.

2. Reward yourself every single time you make the tiny step in the right direction.

Michal Stawicki:

1. Prevent problems with motivation by setting the right goals and tweaking your actions to ensure results.

2. Create a plan and track your results from day one.

3. Ask yourself if your problems aren't the result of low energy levels. Take a nap to improve your performance.

4. Journal and/or meditate to become more aware of when you rationalize your temptation to give up.

5. Change your personal philosophy by changing the resources you consume (books, blogs, podcasts,

etc.), the people you interact with and your inner thoughts.

Hung Pham:

1. If you're suffering from depression or addiction, set your prejudices aside and seek professional help.

2. When working on big goals, look for the small wins. They add up to the bigger wins.

3. Re-prioritize what is most important and cut away distractions.

4. Nothing hard ever came easy to anyone. Struggle is a part of the process.

Epilogue

I wrote this book with one goal in mind – to help you understand what affects persistence and how to become a grittier person. If my book helped you push through the obstacles and overcome the short-term feeling of discouragement, I consider my job done.

Please don't discount the importance of the first chapter, though. Persistence is deemed the most important quality of successful people, yet the key is to apply the power of your grit to the things that are right in your unique situation.

There have been many times in my life where I followed the wrong path. By giving up things that weren't right for me, I gained more time and energy to focus on the things that were right to me.

That's why I started this book talking about when to quit. As Richard Koch points out in his book "Living the 80/20 Way," if you go for the right activities, you can work effortlessly and achieve a great deal.

If you've already discovered the right things for you, I hope the advice I shared with you in this book will serve you for the rest of your life.

The crucial things to remember:

1. Utilize the power of routines to make your behaviors automated. The less resistance you feel to work on your goals, the less likely you are to give up.

2. Work on your mental toughness by making yourself uncomfortable.

3. Focus on the results and don't disregard the power of proper rest. Even the top performers don't practice for more than four and a half hour a day.

4. Identify how you sabotage yourself and learn how to deal with these behaviors.

5. Become a more resilient person by learning how to adapt to changes and solving problems.

6. Be relentless. Use the five techniques mentioned in Chapter 7 to stick to your goals.

7. Become aware of the most common mistakes people make when working on their goals and avoid them in your life.

Practice the art of persistence, and I know without a doubt you'll achieve your goals and change your life for the better.

Download This Book in Other Formats

I want to thank you for buying my book and offer you access to my book in three additional formats: MOBI, EPUB and PDF.

Click the link below to receive it:

http://www.profoundselfimprovement.com/grit

In addition to getting "Grit," you'll also have an opportunity to get my new books for free, enter giveaways and receive other valuable emails from me.

Again, here's the link to sign up:

http://www.profoundselfimprovement.com/grit

Could You Help?

I'd love to hear your opinion about my book. In the world of book publishing, there are few things more valuable than honest reviews from a wide variety of readers.

Your review will help other readers find out whether my book is for them. It will also help me reach more readers by increasing the visibility of my book.

About Martin Meadows

Martin Meadows is the pen name of an author who has dedicated his life to personal growth. He constantly reinvents himself by making drastic changes in his life.

Over the years, he has regularly fasted for over 40 hours, taught himself two foreign languages, lost over 30 pounds in 12 weeks, ran several businesses in various industries, took ice-cold showers and baths, lived on a small tropical island in a foreign country for several months, and wrote a 400-page long novel's worth of short stories in one month.

Yet, self-torture is not his passion. Martin likes to test his boundaries to discover how far his comfort zone goes.

His findings (based both on his personal experience and scientific studies) help him improve his life. If you're interested in pushing your limits and learning how to become the best version of yourself, you'll love Martin's works.

You can read his books here:

http://www.amazon.com/author/martinmeadows.

---

[i] Duckworth A., Peterson C., Matthews M. D., Kelly D. R., "Grit: Perseverance and Passion for Long-Term Goals." *Journal of Personality and Social Psychology* 2007; 92 (6): 1087–101.

ii Godin S., *The Dip: The Extraordinary Benefits of Knowing When to Quit (and When to Stick)*, 2011.

iii Arkes H. R., Ayton P. "The sunk cost and Concorde effects: Are humans less rational than lower animals?" *Psychological Bulletin* 1999; 125 (5): 591–600.

iv Koch R., *Living the 80/20 Way, New Edition: Work Less, Worry Less, Succeed More, Enjoy More*, 2011.

v King S., *On Writing: A Memoir of the Craft*, 2000.

vi http://lifehacker.com/281626/jerry-seinfelds-productivity-secret, Web. February 25th, 2015.

vii Crust L., Clough P. J., "Developing Mental Toughness: From Research to Practice." *Journal of Sport Psychology in Action* 2011; 2 (1).

viii Ross E., Goodall S., Stevens A., Harris I. "Time Course of Neuromuscular Changes during Running in Well-Trained Subjects." *Medicine & Science in Sports & Exercise* 2010; 42 (6): 1184–1190.

ix Dienstbier R. A. "Arousal and physiological toughness: Implications for mental and physical health". *Psychological Review* 1989; 96: 84–100.

x Dienstbier R. A., LaGuardia R. L., Wilcox N. S. "The relationship of temperament to tolerance of cold and heat: Beyond "cold hands-warm heart." *Motivation and Emotion* 1987, 11: 269–295.

xi Dienstbier R. A. (1984). "The effect of exercise on personality". In M. L. Sachs & G. B. Buffone (Eds.), *Running as therapy: An integrated approach* (pp. 253–272). Lincoln: University of Nebraska Press.

xii http://www.leangains.com/2010/10/top-ten-fasting-myths-debunked.html is a great place to start if you're interested in learning more about the myths associated with fasting.

xiii Tang Y. Y., Lu Q., Geng X., Stein E. A., Yang Y., Posner M. I. (2010). "Short-term meditation induces white matter changes in the anterior cingulate." *Proceedings of the National Academy of Sciences* 2010; 107 (35): 15649–52.

[xiv] https://nccih.nih.gov/health/meditation/overview.htm, Web. February 26th, 2015.

[xv] http://www.inc.com/oscar-raymundo/richard-branson-advice-entrepreneurs-thank-me-for-the-most.html, Web. February 25th, 2015.

[xvi] Westman M., Etzion D., "The impact of vacation and job stress on burnout and absenteeism." *Psychology & Health* 2001; 16 (5).

[xvii] Mah C. D., Mah K. E., Kezirian E. J., Dement W. C., "The effects of sleep extension on the athletic performance of collegiate basketball players." *Sleep* 2011; 34 (7): 943–50.

[xviii] Oaten M., Cheng K. "Academic Examination Stress Impairs Self–Control." *Journal of Social and Clinical Psychology* 2005; 24 (2): 254–279.

[xix] Signal T. L., Gander P. H., Howard A., Brash S., "Scheduled napping as a countermeasure to sleepiness in air traffic controllers." *Journal of Sleep Research* 2009; 18 (1): 11–19.

[xx] http://www.nytimes.com/2013/02/10/opinion/sunday/relax-youll-be-more-productive.html?pagewanted=all, Web. February 26th, 2015.

[xxi] Samuelson W., Zeckhauser R. "Status Quo Bias in Decision Making." *Journal of Risk and Uncertainty* 1988; 1: 7–59.

[xxii] Kahneman D., Tversky A. "Choices, Values, and Frames." *American Psychologist* 1984; 39 (4): 341–350.

[xxiii] Kermer D. A., Driver-Linn E., Wilson T. D., Gilbert D. T. "Loss aversion is an affective forecasting error." *Psychological Science* 2006; 17 (8): 649–653.

[xxiv] Nordgren L. F., van Harreveld F., van der Pligt J. "The restraint bias: how the illusion of self-restraint promotes impulsive behavior." *Psychological Science* 2009; 20 (12): 1523–8.

[xxv] Costa V. D., Tran V. L., Turchi J., Averbeck B. B. "Dopamine modulates novelty seeking behavior during decision making." *Behavioral Neuroscience* 2014; 128 (5): 556–66.

xxvi Duckworth A. L., Peterson C., Matthews M. D., Kelly D. R., "Grit: Perseverance and passion for long-term goals." *Journal of Personality and Social Psychology* 2007, 92 (6): 1087–1101.

xxvii Tugade M. M., Fredrickson B. L., Barrett L. F., "Psychological Resilience and Positive Emotional Granularity: Examining the Benefits of Positive Emotions on Coping and Health." *Journal of Personality* 2004; 72 (6): 1161–1190.

xxviii Lewis M. B., Bowler P. J., "Botulinum toxin cosmetic therapy correlates with a more positive mood." *Journal of Cosmetic Dermatology* 2009; 8 (1).

xxix Emmons R. A., McCullough M. E., "Counting Blessings Versus Burdens: An Experimental Investigation of Gratitude and Subjective Well-Being in Daily Life." *Journal of Personality and Social Psychology* 2003; 84 (2): 377–389.

xxx Seligman M. E., Steen T. A., Park N., Peterson C., "Positive psychology progress: empirical validation of interventions." *The American Psychologist* 2005; 60 (5): 410–21.

xxxi For more information about positive psychology, read: Seligman M. E. P., *Learned Optimism: How to Change Your Mind and Your Life*, 2006.

xxxii Ashraf N., Karlan D., Yin W., "Tying Odysseus to the Mast: Evidence from a Commitment Savings Product in the Philippines." *Quarterly Journal of Economics* 2006; 121 (2): 635–672.

xxxiii Irwin B. C., Scorniaenchi J., Kerr N. L., Eisenmann J. C., Feltz D. L. "Aerobic exercise is promoted when individual performance affects the group: a test of the Kohler motivation gain effect." *Annals of Behavioral Medicine: a Publication of the Society of Behavioral Medicine* 2012; 44 (2): 151–9.

xxxiv Feltz D. L., Irwin B., Kerr N. "Two-player partnered exergame for obesity prevention: using discrepancy in players' abilities as a strategy to motivate physical activity." *Journal of Diabetes Science and Technology* 2012; 6 (4): 820–7.

xxxv Hamilton R. A., Scott D., MacDougall M. P. "Assessing the effectiveness of self-talk interventions on endurance performance". *Journal of Applied Sport Psychology* 2007; 19: 226–239.

xxxvi Polivy J., Herman C. P. (2002). "If at first you don't succeed: False hopes of self-change." *American Psychologist* 2002; 57 (9): 677–689.

xxxvii Pham L. B., Taylor S. E. "From Thought to Action: Effects of Process-Versus Outcome-Based Mental Simulations on Performance." *Personality and Social Psychology Bulletin* 1999; 25 (2): 250–260.

xxxviii Armor D. A., Taylor S. E., "The Effects of Mindset on Behavior: Self-Regulation in Deliberative and Implemental Frames of Mind." *Personality and Social Psychology Bulletin* 2003; 29 (1): 86–95.

xxxix Hall E. G., Erffmeyer E. S., "The effect of visuo-motor behavior rehearsal with videotaped modeling on free throw accuracy of intercollegiate female basketball players." *Journal of Sport Psychology* 1983; 5 (3): 343–346.

xl Vasquez N. A., Buehler R., "Seeing Future Success: Does Imagery Perspective Influence Achievement Motivation?" *Personality and Social Psychology Bulletin* 2007; 33 (10): 1392–1405.

xli Read Will Bowen's book "A Complaint Free World: How to Stop Complaining and Start Enjoying the Life You Always Wanted" for more information about this experiment.

xlii Blake T., *Three Simple Steps: A Map to Success in Business and Life*, 2012.

xliii http://fortune.com/2012/08/09/colleagues-complaining-why-you-need-to-tune-it-out/, Web. February 27th, 2015.

52691184R00072

Made in the USA
Lexington, KY
07 June 2016